Manual  the
LIGHT

John-Roger

Mandeville Press
Los Angeles, California

Published by Mandeville Press
P.O. Box 513935
Los Angeles, CA 90051-1935
e-mail: jrbooks@msia.org

Printed in the United States of America
ISBN 0-914829-13-0

FOREWORD

The "Light", which is another term for the "Holy Spirit", is one of the basic concepts of the organization known as "The Movement of Spiritual Inner Awareness." This book expresses, in a child-like fashion, the many facets and uses of this force or energy.

The Movement of Spiritual Inner Awareness, whose membership is now world-wide, is located in Los Angeles, California, and is headed by founder and spiritual teacher, John-Roger

More information concerning this movement can be obtained by writing to:

M.S.I.A.
Box 3935
Los Angeles, Ca. 90051

Well, I guess, first of all, I should tell you what this thing called the LIGHT is, before you start using it.

Let me introduce you to the folks.

Cause, you see, this
LIGHT happens to be
the most powerful force
around — and it's really
not something to be
played with.

(although you'll find it has a
great sense of humor, sometimes.)

You see, what it really
is, is the manifestation
of the Supreme GOD,
on this level.

It's the HOLY SPIRIT.

It's what GOD uses when
He wants to get something
done here on Earth.

GOD

Now, there's some of this LIGHT inside of everybody already (it's what gives us LIFE.) But there's also a whole big endless reserve of it in the Highest Realm of LIGHT, that you can call on to use.

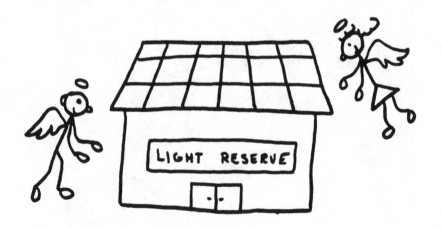

Now, there aren't too many
people around who can
actually s͟e͟e͟ the LIGHT,
cause you don't see it
with your regular physical
eyes — you have to look
through your spiritual eye.
(also called your third eye)

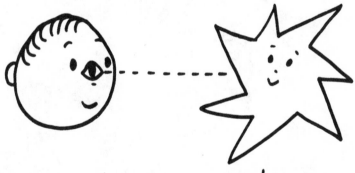

And most people don't even
know they have one of
those yet.

But, just because you can't see the LIGHT, doesn't mean it doesn't exist.

(You can't see GRAVITY, either, you know.)

But then, you don't have to go completely on FAITH, either, cause there are a whole lot of ways of going about PROVING its existence to yourself;

I'm an empiricist, myself.

and that's what this manual is all about.

Just going around blindly
believing in some thing
doesn't work too good,
cause we all got rational
minds, and so I guess
GOD wants us to use
them.

GOD

See what
you can do
with this.

And, anyway, it sure is more comfortable when all parts of us understand what's going on.

Hey, what's all this crazy stuff about that "Light" you keep talking about?

Well, now maybe you're
wondering why you might ever
even want to use the LIGHT.

Well, it's to help you help
GOD do GOD's work —
which is what we all want
to do, in the long run,
anyway, don't we?

I don't think we have a choice.

Even if we _do_ have a choice, I think its FUN doing GOD's work, cause you know what? It sure does give you a GOOD FEELING.

It makes you so HIGH, and so filled to overbrimming with LAUGHTER and JOY and LOVE for everybody and everything that you could almost BURST!

So, who wouldn't want to help do GOD's work, in spreading all this good stuff around?

That's why I'm going to tell you some ways in which you can use the LIGHT, and give you some tips, so it can work for you.

The first thing to remember to do, is when you call in the LIGHT, always remember to add the 'safety clause':

"FOR THE HIGHEST GOOD OF ALL CONCERNED."

This is because there's another Light, that comes from the negative realms, called the "MAGNETIC LIGHT", that isn't the HOLY SPIRIT, and this can be used indiscriminately for selfish means.

(either consciously or unconsciously)

And using the MAGNETIC LIGHT can be very dangerous, cause it can bring with it a whole bunch of KARMA for you.

(It's the one that people into magic, and that kind of thing, use.)

So, if you always say, "FOR THE HIGHEST GOOD OF ALL CONCERNED", you automatically bring in the HOLY SPIRIT LIGHT, cause it's the only thing that knows what's for the highest good of all concerned.

Now, you don't always have to say all those words : you don't even have to think all of them. But if you just think the CONCEPT, the LIGHT will get the message.

So, here's some ways you can use the LIGHT.

One good way to use it is for yourself.

Yeah, let's start with me.

You know, like if you're
feeling way down in the
dumps, for example, and
your emotions are running
all over you,

and you don't know how
to get out of the
mess.

If you call the LIGHT in, it can really alter the situation for you. Like it might just clarify your mind, so that you can suddenly see clearly what's really going on—

and then get yourself out of it.

Or, it might have some-
body else enter into the
picture, and have <u>him</u>
show you what's really
going on — and how you
can get out of it.

why don't you
just stand up?

Or, it just might make the whole mess you're in even WORSE for you, so that you'll just have to BURST your way free of it, out of sheer desperation —

and then be able to stand back and look at it.

You see, there are all sorts of ways the LIGHT might work in this kind of situation.

But, the thing you got to remember is that

YOU CAN'T TELL THE LIGHT WHAT TO DO, OR HOW TO DO IT.

You can, but it isn't
going to work. Cause
when it's called on, it
works in the way it knows
how for the highest good.

And there's a pretty good
chance you don't always
know what's for the highest
good.

You mean,
you know more
than I do?

A lot of times we like to think we do, but it's pretty evident in looking at things with HINDSIGHT,

that we didn't.

And sometimes you're
going to be so happy
the LIGHT didn't do
what you wanted it to,
cause wow what a
mess things would
have been, if it h<u>ad</u>.

whew!

Another situation you might
want to use the LIGHT
in is say where you're
in a fight with someone,
and you're both hurting each
other and hurting your-
selves, and knowing it...

but not knowing how to
stop it.

Well, the way the LIGHT
might work in this kind
of situation would be to
suddenly make you start
laugh_i_ng —

which, as you know, can
really spoil a good
fight.

Or, it might suddenly make you cry, which would make you both go through all kinds of changes, and in some way alter the situation — like maybe making your opponent realize what he's doing,

and say he's sorry.

Or, the LIGHT might even
make the fight get so bad,
that you both start feeling
so terrible, and then
suddenly realize toge_ther
what an awful mess you're
in —

and you'd better take back
what you said, before you
start killing each other.

You see, it all depends on who's involved, what state of SPIRITUAL EVOLVEMENT you're at, and what kinds of LESSONS each of

 you are supposed to

be learning for your

HIGHEST GOOD.

Sometimes, the exact same thing that you're calling the LIGHT in to change is exactly what is needed for your highest good – so absolutely NOTHING CHANGES.

And that's a good
thing to remember, so
you don't get mad at
the LIGHT for not
helping you.

You stupid
Light!

If nothing seems to happen, then it's a good thing to ask the LIGHT for clarification of the situation, so you can understand what's going on.

okay, so what's going on here?

I'm glad you asked.

Another situation you
might want to use the
LIGHT in could be
when nothing in particular
seems to be wrong, but
you're just feeling out
of BALANCE, somehow.

This kind of thing happens
a lot when your three selves
aren't in agreement about
something, and they're pushing
on each other.

You see, you got three selves
inside of you, that your SOUL
is using to gain experiences
through.

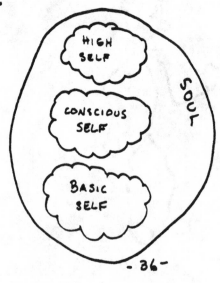

And even though they all work together as a unit, they are all separate, and have separate functions and ideas of how things should be run.

The self that we all
know about and see
is the

CONSCIOUS
SELF.

I'm obvious

This is the one who directs the actions of the person, who uses the brain, and makes all the choices.

It's the one we usually identify with, before we realize we have two other selves too.

Then there's the self
called the

BASIC SELF.

This self is in charge of
your body and your
emotions.

Now, this is the one that
seems to cause a lot of
trouble for us. Until you
find out who this one is,
and let it know that you
(as your conscious self)
are BOSS, and that it is
going to have to go along
with what you decide — it's
going to be tough going.

See here,
now.

Cause, in lots of cases,
people have let their
basic selves run their
lives for a long time,

Come on, let's
go get revenge
on him - and
then eat a whole
apple pie to
celebrate it!

and it's like taking a
great big favorite toy
away from a child, when
you say, "Look, Basic Self,
I'm Boss here now, and
you're going to have to do
what I say."

Now, this doesn't mean that you have to be mean to it and order it around.

Not at all.
You have to be STRICT,
but also LOVING, cause
you got to have its
cooperation —

Let's do this together.

Seeing as it's the one that has control of your body and your emotions. and it can get back at you pretty good, if it wants to.

Alright for you! I'm going to give you a stomach ache!

So, what you should do,
is treat it like a
BABY, where you guide
its life in a loving,
understanding way.

Then, there's the

HIGH SELF,

who really doesn't get involved with all this silly stuff that goes on between your Conscious Self and your Basic Self.

I'm above it all.

It stays very NEUTRAL on all issues. Its job is to attempt to steer you onto your spiritual path, cause it knows what you came in to do in this lifetime,

and what you have to do to get back to the SOUL REALM, where we're all headed.

But, if you (as your conscious self) choose to ignore it, it's okay, it doesn't get mad and yell at you or bring lightning down on you, or anything.

It just goes on, UNDISTURBED, in doing its job of bringing about opportunity after opportunity to help you learn and understand what GOD is all about and what you're really doing in this funny place called Earth.

So, anyway, when you've got these three selves inside of you, going about their business, sometimes it's hard to keep them all in line and in BALANCE.

So it's a good thing to call in the LIGHT to help straighten you out.

Sometimes, what might happen at this point would be that you'd suddenly get very sleepy, so you go and take a nap,

and then wake up, feeling really good, cause you worked out the balance in the dream state.

Or, maybe what might happen is someone will suddenly walk in the door who needs a lot of help.

And so you stop thinking
about yourself altogether
and start thinking about
her, and HELPING her.

And then you realize
after all that, YOU feel
pretty straightened out.

Helping
sure feels
good.

See, what happens is the LIGHT will use all Kinds of methods to pull you up into a higher state of spiritual awareness, and that's what makes you feel better, always.

But depending on you and the situation, it will use different methods.

Another way to use the
LIGHT is to send it to
other people, when
they're in some kind of
trouble. And this gets
to be a neat thing,
to watch it work.

Gee, I didn't
really think
it was going
to work.

There are different ways in which you can send it to someone else.

One good way is to first of all call on it for that person's highest good, and then with your imagination (which is what you have to use at first), feel it come into you, and then flow out of you from the area where your third eye is.

Then imagine it flowing straight to that person, and swirling around him, and awakening his spiritual awareness about himself.

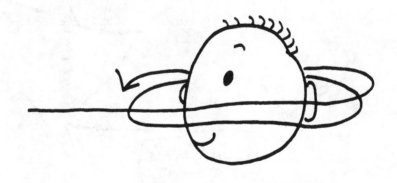

One thing you really got to watch, though, is not to tell the LIGHT specifically what you want it to do, cause you might not even know what's wrong with the person.

OK, Light, here's what I want you to do. First of all...

Say, for example, you have
a friend who seems
miserable with a runny
nose and sneezing and
coughing,

and you think, "Oh, Light,
please go to my friend
and clear up her cold
for her highest good."

And then, NOTHING HAPPENS, she's still just as sick.

Well, don't blame the
LIGHT. You know
there's a very good
chance your friend
has an ALLERGY, and
not a cold, at all.

oh.

So, what you got to do, is let the LIGHT make the diagnosis of the sick- ness, and let it take care of it the best way it knows how.

LIGHT, M.D.

(And since the LIGHT has perfect knowledge, it knows some pretty good ways.)

Another thing to remember
when you're sending the
LIGHT to some one else,
is that it's really nice to
picture the LIGHT returning
to you, after it's finished
with them, so you get
in on some of the action,
too.

You'll know when it hits you,
Cause you can feel it, if
you really tune in.
Sometimes it'll suddenly
make you smile, or even
giggle!

TICKLE,
TICKLE!

What's really neat about
Practicing using the
LIGHT is that even if
you can't understand
what's going on at first,
it's still a lot of fun to
practice with it, anyway.

Cause you find yourself
going through so many neat
changes, and feeling so
much LOVE for people —
and realizing how you're
really one with GOD, and
that life is so beautiful.

And you'll find yourself
believing in the LIGHT,
even despite yourself, sometimes...

I don't know why
I believe in this
silly stuff, but...

Because that SOMETHING-
inside of you is starting
to awaken, and is
telling you, "Yes, the
LIGHT is for real, and
you and it are one and
the same thing."

And pretty soon, it's so fantastic, cause your

BELIEVING

starts turning into

KNOWING

And at that point, you can't hardly believe it, cause your whole life has changed.

And you know you're really
going some place, and it's
a beautiful place. You've
been trying to get there
for so long, and now
you've finally found out
how to get there.
Thanks to the LIGHT.

And you know what?
You're going to find
yourself saying,

IT
REALLY
DOES
WORK!

Books by John-Roger

Spiritual Warrior—The Art of Spiritual Success
Inner Worlds of Meditation
The Tao of Spirit
Forgiveness: The Key to the Kingdom
The Christ Within & The Disciples of Christ
    with the Cosmic Christ Calendar
Dream Voyages
Walking with the Lord
God Is Your Partner
Q&A from the Heart
Passage Into Spirit
Relationships—The Art of Making Life Work
Loving—Each Day
Wealth & Higher Consciousness
The Power Within You
The Spiritual Promise
The Spiritual Family
The Sound Current
The Signs of the Times
The Way Out Book
Sex, Spirit & You
Possessions, Projections & Entities
The Path to Mastership
Music is the Message
The Master Chohans of the Color Rays
The Journey of a Soul
Dynamics of the Lower Self
Drugs
The Consciousness of Soul
Buddha Consciousness
Blessings of Light
Baraka
Awakening Into Light

For further information, please contact:
Mandeville Press®
P.O. Box 513935
Los Angeles, CA 90051-1935
(213) 737-4055

About the Author

Since 1963, John-Roger has traveled all over the world, lecturing, teaching, and assisting people who want to create a life of greater health, happiness, peace, and prosperity and a greater awakening to the Spirit within. His humor and practical wisdom have benefited thousands and lightened many a heart.

In the course of this work, he has given over 5,000 seminars, many of which are televised nationally on "That Which Is." He has also written more than 35 books, including co-authoring two *New York Times* best-sellers.

The common thread throughout all John-Roger's work is loving, opening to the highest good of all, and the awareness that God is abundantly present and available.

If you've enjoyed this book, you may want to explore and delve more deeply into what John-Roger has shared about this subject and other related topics. See the bibliography for a selection of study materials. For an even wider selection of study materials and more information on John-Roger's teachings through MSIA, please contact us at:

MSIA®
P.O. Box 513935
Los Angeles, CA 90051-1935
(213) 737-4055
soul@msia.org
http://www.msia.org